Be Weird, Make Money: Halloween

Kimberly Stewart

Table of Contents

Introduction

Welcome to Be Weird, Make Money: Halloween. My name is Kimberly Stewart and I'm glad you picked up this book to read about some small business ideas. I'm guessing you're probably either interested in starting a business or adding a Halloween aspect to your existing business. Being weird and making money is all about expressing your inner nerd and what better way to do that than with a holiday like Halloween? I have found that creative people don't always think in terms of how to make money with their talent or, if they have, they haven't figured out how to do so yet. It can feel weird to get paid for having fun, doing what you love most, or doing stuff that comes easy to you. But I promise it can happen. I've seen it happen.

According to the National Retail Federation in 2014, $7.4 billion dollars was spent on Halloween. The breakdown of those numbers is:

$2.8 billion dollars on people costumes

$350 million dollars just on pet costumes

$2.2 billion dollars on candy

$2 billion dollars on decorations

$360 million dollars just on greeting cards - now this statistic really floored me, and when I saw that I thought, "Who buys these things, really?" But then I thought over the past couple of years and there are friends who know I'm really into

Halloween that have sent me Halloween cards. I guess I just never really thought a whole lot about it.

$300 to 500 million dollars on haunted attractions.

This is BIG BUSINESS, friends!

But what if you don't know how you would be able to compete with one of the large companies that dominate those categories (or at least you don't want to start there)? What if you want a specialized, unique, niche - a boutique kind of business? Well I'm here to get you thinking about Halloween-based businesses and to make you realize that small can be beautiful. It doesn't mean that you can't go big but it's a nice place to start. You can find out a lot of information while you're still small, such as: do you even like it? Does it work the way you thought it would? What problems didn't you anticipate (cost/time needed/the product doesn't work/etc.)? You can make a lot of mistakes experimenting with dry runs when your business is small and it's not as embarrassing. You know, the saying goes, "Dream big, but start small".

Alright, so who am I? I am a small business idea consultant. Basically, I help people put together their ideas of how to start a business. I help them identify their goals - how to go after them and create lives that they love. I brainstorm different ways for people to combine their interests and talents and then create completely unique individualized businesses that will be profitable.

Since 2003 I have been a Success Team Leader - which is a creation by my friend and mentor Barbara Sher. She is the author of a several books, but my favorites are "I Could Do Anything If I Only Knew What It Was" and "Refuse to Choose". The last one, "Refuse To Choose," is such a wonderful book because it brings up the idea that you don't have to choose just one thing. It gives you the permission and the necessary steps to take if you want to do lots of things. You know, there's a lot of people out there who have many, often diverse interests and they think, "Oh my gosh, what if I want to do too many things?" Well, Barbara shows you that there's no such thing. I have a lot of fun meeting with small groups of people to help them identify their goals. As a Success Team Leader I meet with these people for two months to provide structure and accountability for reaching these goals.

In 2009, I studied with Dr. Valerie Young, author of "Secret Thoughts of Successful Women" and became a Profiting From Your Passions consultant. It's very similar to what I do as a Success Team Leader, only I work with people one-on-one and I love doing that as well.

I've also been mentored by Barbara Winter, she's the author of "Making a Living Without a Job," which is a fantastic book - I can't recommend it highly enough and she and her book and classes have really helped me become who I am today in doing what I do.

Most importantly (for this book), I'm a lifelong Halloween enthusiast. I was that kid who in April and May started getting excited for Halloween, thinking about what my costume would be for that year. I always thought I was just the weird one. Then, in 2006, I went to Opus Fest (a dark arts fantasy festival in Denver) - they had a whole wing dedicated to just Halloween and horror workshops and I realized this was a thing. You know, they had workshops on costuming and makeup and how to make props and it was just amazing. I realized I wasn't the only one out there! That led me to find Hauntforum.com and Garage of Evil (a great site for prop how-to's). I joined my local Garage of Evil group out here in Colorado and we get together throughout the year; we make props and it's so much fun. I often find myself saying, "Wow! For a group of people who like to scare people, you're an awfully friendly bunch!" I was at HAuNTcon in January of 2014 giving a talk about this subject and I found that it was the same there, too. Everyone was really awesome, people were really enthusiastic about Halloween and it was great to not feel alone.

Recently, I figured, "Why not put these two things together, my love of Halloween and my love of small business ideas?" As I was getting ready to go speak about Halloween businesses at HAuNTcon (in 2014)I realized that most business classes offered were how to run a haunt - a big professional haunted attraction - and nobody was talking about little guy businesses. Well, that's what I do. Let's get started!

<u>Overview</u>

We're going to start out by looking at income generating
opportunities. These are places that you can look for
inspiration. So, if you're not entirely sure about your
business idea yet, we will begin with some suggestions
of places to start. Then we're going to discuss what I
have identified as the Seven Paths to Profits which are:
services, products, information products, landlord, mail
order, bricks and mortar businesses, and
entertainment/performance. I'll show you what examples
of these ideas might look like. I have highlighted people
and businesses in each category for us to explore what
they have done with their ideas and hopefully use this
experience to come up with our own! But, I don't want
you to get discouraged. If I start talking about an idea

and you think, "Dang-it! That's what I wanted to do!"
don't worry. If somebody is already doing it, it means
there's a market for it. Also they might be in a totally
different part of the country. Competition is healthy and
it's good; you might be able to serve different markets
and so there might not be the bad side of competition. As
I go along, we'll look at some untapped niches. These
are areas where I see gaps in these categories – and
maybe *you* will be the person to fill these places! I want
to be clear that none of these ideas is likely to bring you
a full-time income right away or possibly even ever, but
that's okay! When I was in the beginning stages of
writing this book, someone asked me, "How is a
Halloween business going to support someone all year"?
Well, it might not. But who says it has to? That's the
beauty of this; how much you make is all up to you. You

choose how much you want to work, what scale you want to bring to your business, and what you want out of the experience. Bottom line: I don't want any of you to go quit your job. You don't need that kind of stress when you're just starting out. If it helps, think of your current job as what Barbara Sher calls, a "Good Enough Job" (which she defines as one that doesn't work you more than 40 hours a week, isn't toxic/super stressful, and provides enough money to cover the bills), or more poetically, "A Subsidy to the Arts". Business coach Suzanne Evans says, "Think of your job as your business loan."

Once we figure out your idea, we'll discuss is how to get the word out about this new endeavor of yours! Pinterest and social media tools are incredibly powerful and a growing number of people are turning to these places for inspiration.

Chapter One: Income Generating Opportunities

So, what if you think this sounds cool and all, but have no idea where to get started? Where can you look for ideas and inspiration? Fear not! I will show you five different places that you can investigate to find your perfect idea. You don't have to think of the opportunities separately either. You can combine several of these categories to make your idea specific and unique.

1. *Problems, complaints, and threats.* Basically all business is learning how to solve problems. If you pay attention, you can see where people are

struggling as well as possible solutions. Listen for complaints about existing businesses or services. Or, listen when you hear people saying, "Why doesn't somebody do this?" and that's a great place to start. For example, I met a gal in Pennsylvania named Delia who owns Delia's Special Effects and Makeup Shop. In addition to selling makeup, she hosts several special effects makeup classes a year. She is also a makeup artist who works on feature films. One of the problems and complaints that she encounters frequently is how bad mouth blood (fake blood used around the mouth) tastes. So she actually developed a whole line of blood, including a line of edible mouth blood. She can customize the color and flavoring of the mouth blood. For example, you can get chocolate, strawberry, or chocolate strawberry; it's amazing and they taste really good. In this way, she responded to a complaint, found a way to solve the problem, and filled a need.

2. *Trend.* If you can attach your business to a trend, it's a terrific way to immediately get attention in your market. What's hot? Or more importantly, what's *going* to be hot? Don't jump on the train tracks after the train has left the station. You don't need a crystal ball, but a keen observation of your market. Think zombies, (or, depending on when you are reading this, whatever this year's current trends are) - or one trend that I think we'd all like to stake in the heart is sparkly

vampires. Pay attention to what's big these days or what's up and coming and that may be a great way to shape your business.

3. *Demographic groups*. You are targeting your business to these people. Who are the people who are looking to buy your products, services, or ideas? Are they fellow haunters who are thinking about Halloween all year? Are they mainstream people who like Halloween only in October? Is it kids? Teenagers? The older crowd? Are they people who like extreme gore and thrilling experiences, or are they those who are looking for more family-friendly fare? Who are you looking to attract? It is important to know this information so you can evaluate what those

people like, what they buy, look at their trends - that sort of thing. Then, you can figure out how to design your business based on that. We'll talk more about this later, but start thinking about who else is interested in selling to your market. Are these people, businesses, or sponsors who you could team up with to help get the word out? This can be especially helpful as you're just getting started and can likely use all the help you can get. What are you doing that complements what they're doing or fills a need?

4. *Interests or hobbies.* So, you're here reading this because you love Halloween. But each of us Halloween fiends has different things that we like to do - whether it's crafting or performing or

writing - that's where you want to start. It's kind of like: how do you find your crowd, your people? For example: Do you quilt? Would you be interested in making monster-themed quilt patterns? Or are you into electronics? What if you taught people how to program 3-axis talking skulls to sing along to a song? It's all about finding that sweet spot where what you love to do meets what someone needs and is willing to pay for.

5. *Personal experience.* A great way to come up with ideas for a business is to share mistakes you've made or successes that you've had. I'm going to talk more about information products later, but I know a lot of people (my Home

Haunter friends, as well as pros) run into problems with fire marshals and code enforcement and that sort of thing. If you had a problem with the fire marshal and you figured out how to overcome the obstacles, you can put that information together and sell it to people who might need it. Kind of like, "Don't do what I did" or, "Here's how I overcame this struggle." Any one of these, or a combination of them, is going to help you figure out where to start and where the money might be. Another way you can think about this is what are you an expert in? Have you developed wicked technique for a prop you'd be willing to share (for a price)? Are you a town historian or do you just have a lot of love/pride for your hometown? You could design

walking tours, cemetery tours, books/booklets of
your town or region's history particularly as it
pertains to Halloween, autumn, or ghosts and
hauntings. Don't worry if you're not the
performing type, you could sell your information
as pamphlets for self-guided tours, or share
profits with entertainers who take people on
them.

Some ways that you might look at blending these
income-generating opportunities might include:

What *trends* are big with your demographic?

What are the biggest problems with _____
(costumes, decorations, etc) your demographic faces and
needs help with?

What personal experience (good or bad) coincides with a trend that you could share?

What non-Halloween hobbies or interests do you have that you could bring a Halloween flavor to? (Remember when we talked about a quilting or electronics hobby?)

Chapter Two: Services

Services are great because they're easy to start, generally speaking, and often they have low start-up costs. It's basically you going to do something for someone else, and you might not need a whole lot of equipment to begin. That makes these services portable, which is nice because then you're not stuck in one location. The author of, "The Popcorn Report", Faith Popcorn is a business economist who looks at trends. She said the biggest trend for the 2000's is *time*. Time is the hot commodity: if you can save someone time and energy by helping them do something that's not in their skill set, you will always have business.

So, what might some of these services look like?

Makeup, particularly for Halloween, is a big deal. Not everyone knows how to do special effects makeup or really intricate makeup. But if it's one thing you really love to do, all it's going to cost you is a simple makeup kit to get started and you can hire yourself out for parties, either for kids or adults. You could go to different events, do face painting or tutorials/ how-to's. If there's one kind of makeup that you really like to do, you can have people pay you to show them how to do that particular technique. Love to do zombie makeup? Is there a zombie event/crawl/walk happening nearby? Is there a Halloween parade happening? Check with the organizers to see if you can set up a table. You could make up participants or spectators and maybe sell little, inexpensive costume parts (think animal ears and noses) that folks might be willing to pick up for themselves or for the kids not in the parade.

This next one is one of those untapped niches that I've seen. Has anyone ever seen the signs that go up before Christmas, "Will hang lights for Christmas," and "Decorate your house for Christmas?" Well I got thinking - wouldn't it be fun if you could decorate other people's houses for Halloween? There are a lot of people with money and interest but not necessarily the time or skills to do a great yard haunt or Halloween party decorations. What if you had props at your disposal and you had a couple of different scenes? You could ask people their budget, and what theme they want to go with, such as a cemetery or carnival, for example. Then make an appointment to set up, as well as a tear down date. I remember thinking about this when I lived in an apartment where I didn't really have the space to decorate I thought, "If I just had a friend who had a house that I could go decorate, it would be such a blast." Well, what if you could make money at it? Speaking of making money, some of the folks who do this for Christmas businesses can make six figures in six weeks. Just take that in - $100,000 or more in six weeks just by decorating people's houses and businesses for Christmas! And so, while doing this for Halloween might not be that big of a thing yet, it could be. One more thought about this, don't get stuck on the idea of residential houses, what about approaching local businesses for their decorating? Think about it. If you're already doing the Christmas decorating, why not consider adding this on as an additional service for your existing clients (or as way to get new ones). Or perhaps you could find the folks in your town who are doing the Christmas decorating and ask to team up with them. Or maybe just take them out for coffee and find out how they got started, what advice they have for you, and maybe how you can help them expand their business (by adding Halloween to their service).

How about being a Halloween party or event planner (we'll get to Halloween wedding planner soon, that's a subject that can have its own section)? What a great way to boost your business in what is likely a quiet time. The wedding and summer party season is over but it's not time for winter holiday parties yet!

So this is a great opportunity for you to work together with different venues that may have a lot of openings on their schedules. You could plan parties for people who have the budget, have the interest, but they just don't have the time or maybe even the skill set. Not everybody is really good at planning a party - which is why party and event planners exist! You may be beginning to sense a theme here, but if you're not a professional planner, there might be one you could team up with for the season. The point I want to make is that if this is not your full-time gig, and you're not sure about if you want it to be, teaming up or partnering with people is a great way to "date" an idea without "marrying" it.

You could run classes in whatever you're really good at. For example you could talk about or teach subjects such as props making, costumes, or even baking (gluten-free, anyone?). Here's where you start thinking about your demographics - *who* do you want to teach this to? If you're teaching fellow haunters and Halloween enthusiasts, you might need a little bit more advanced or interesting makeup or props. Mainstream people might just want to do something basic, which is fine because everyone starts somewhere. Do you want to teach kids (after school or community groups) or adults (parents, child free, adult learning centers)? The sky's the limit with this - whatever you really love to do is something you can teach.

What if you are really interested in ghost/haunted area/building tours? It should go without saying you need to get all the proper permissions to do so, if a program is not already in place. Given the popularity of TV shows and movies with interest in seeing ghosts, this is certainly an area where you could make some money. The folks over at HauntedAmericaTours.com have fantastic article titled, "How to Start Your Very Own Ghost Tour" that is worth investigating if this is what you want to get started! According to them, the basics of starting a ghost tour are:

1) Be professional- don't bad mouth other tours- work *with* them and refer your patrons.

2) Find out about the haunted places in your area. This is personally my favorite part! Think about how you can make your tour unique- either by specializing the information (see about niche cemetery tours below), or by how making it fun

for the people on your tour. Maybe you could bring ghost hunting equipment for the patrons to use? Or, as the Haunted America article mentions, one tour offered a séance at a stop along the way. Be creative!

3) Advertise- people can't come on your tour if they don't know you exist. Work with your local media, historical groups, and hotel concierges, to give away tickets to tours and help boost your signal.

4) As mentioned earlier: GET PERMISSION! Talk to your local authorities to see if you need permits or licenses to run tours.

5) Figure out what you're going to charge. An average price will be around $10-15 per person, but take your locale into consideration when setting your rates. Big cities are more likely to bring in higher rates, whereas smaller towns may not support that amount. Don't forget about cemetery tours, either. A few years ago, I went on a tour at Riverside Cemetery one of Denver's most historically significant cemeteries) hosted by a friend from my local Garage of Evil group. The theme of the tour we went on was historical famous women of Denver and it was fascinating. Our guide had this huge binder full of information about the cemetery, organized by the various tours that she would do. The cemetery was huge and it was fascinating how many pieces

of trivia she had! I'd like to go back and see all of her tours. Are there historical cemeteries in your area? Is there a historical society, or cemetery preservationists you could find out from, and perhaps team up with?

Another exciting idea popping up in some areas is doing haunted attraction tours. Depending on the size of your town or city, you could tour by bus or limo. You could get discount VIP tickets by buying in bulk. Get tickets for a bunch of local haunts and everybody can just hop in the vehicle and not have to worry about driving, parking, getting lost, or standing in line for too long! Everyone could just go through the haunt, and then come back out and head to the next one! There are many people who would appreciate this service willingly pay for it. What if you ended the night with a pub crawl-with rides home from the drivers of the bus/limo? This last option might be best with small groups. You might also get the local haunts involved as sponsors.

Another untapped niche might be a creepy location scout. You could find different locations that are creepy in nature and maybe not commonplace. Maybe not a location where everyone is going to have their wedding reception, but that would be a cool place to have a Halloween party. There's a great book called <u>Creepy Crawls: A Horror Fiend's Travel Guide</u> by Leon Marcelo. While the nature of his speech is a little cheesy it's a delightful read. It's basically a travel guide that is based on different horror movie locations or locations that are big in horror literature. What if you could find these places and set up tours or events? If you were to reserve these spots, for people you knew were looking for them, you could make some money by being the coordinator.

Are you an excellent baker with a talent for accommodating different food allergies/needs? Or perhaps are you a baker with a healthy focus? There are a lot of families who have a range of food considerations- from allergies, such as needing to be gluten-free, to those looking to cut down on sugar (yes, even at Halloween!). Many people may not have yet learned the skills of baking for these specific diets or needs. Teaching candy making, gluten-free baking, or making healthy Halloween treats could be really lucrative. This is where Pinterest will be one of your best friends, because this is where moms, in particular, are looking for this information. You could make money from advertisers on your blog, sponsors for ingredients or baking kits you are demonstrating or by linking your page to Pinterest to build traffic. Pinchofyum.com is an incredibly successful food blog that has a whole page dedicated to outlining how (and how much) they make money from their efforts. Alternately, if you wanted to do this in person, you could look for professional kitchens in your area where you can run classes and not have to worry about dealing with health department regulations all alone. You might also consider starting a YouTube recipe/cooking channel if you feel comfortable in front of a camera!

One thing that could be lucrative is making invitations for other people's parties. On Hauntforum, I have seen some of the most lovely, intricate, handcrafted party invitations that users have shared. They are really labors of love, and I have always felt envious of the folks receiving them. While many people have talent, not everyone has the attention to detail and imagination to get the job done. You could work with people planning parties (regular people or perhaps event planners) and either come up with the design for the invitations, or you could just execute the plans that they don't have the time/talent to do. You could come up with a "Standard" couple of options that would simply be customized with their information. Or you could work with them to come up with something totally unique and customized to their party's theme.

Chapter Three: Products

Products are fun because you get to invent and/or make things. You don't always have to come up with things from scratch; you could be improving on products like Delia did with her line of mouth blood. A nice thing about products is, like with Services, they are portable. Unless you have a retail location (which we'll be talking about later), you can take your product to different retail locations or events and sell them there. I've had people say to me, "Well, Kim, I don't have a substantial amount of money to put into production or manufacturing this." While this can be true, never fear, there are options. You can license products. If you can come up with a decent enough prototype you can bring it around to different manufacturers. They'll do the work for you, and you make the money! Even if you can't come up with a prototype there are companies who do nothing but make prototypes. When I was at HAuNTcon I met this guy named Ray Villafane of Villafane Studios and he's known for carving pumpkins. He's developed a product that look like arms and legs made out of vines that you can put on your pumpkins once they're carved. He has some that are creepy and some that are sort of silly. The way his assistant described it to me was basically like Mr. Potato Head for your pumpkin. They were at the Halloween Party Expo (which is a wholesaler show) looking for people to license their product so they could take over production. You may have seen them in this year's Grandin Road Halloween catalog. So don't worry, if you have a product and you're not sure how you'd afford it, there are ways to pay for it and still make money which is pretty cool. Don't rule out crowd funding as way to get money and build interest for your project, either!

With products, there's a wide range of startup costs depending on what you're making. You can start out really on the cheap and recycle products, by going dumpster diving, and recreating things. Or you could go a little higher end depending on whatever it is you're creating. Some of these products might look like props such as coffins, tombstones, skeletons, and all the usual sorts of different props that people might want to put in their house. Once again, I know you're getting the idea, but who is your market? Are these going to be other haunters or are they your next door neighbor? The answer will indicate the types of details you will want to include. Typically, your fellow Halloween enthusiast will be looking for something more over-the-top, whereas a casual decorator might be pleased with something simple and basic.

With some 2.8 billion dollars spent in 2014 just on costumes, clearly there is a huge market for costumes for pets and people. Custom work is where you are going to make your money. And paying attention to trends is one of the most important factors for costumes. Imagine being on the front of the wave with Disney's® Frozen phenomenon? There are plenty of licensors with Disney, so that's not where to focus your energy; no, you want to focus in is with parents who want their little angel to have the best costume in show.

Remember when we talked about problems and demographics as being places to look for ideas? Here is a great example: Magic Wheelchair is a non-profit that creates truly outstanding costumes for kids in wheelchairs. It began with 3 of the founders' 5 children having a condition called Spinal Muscular Atrophy, a form of muscular dystrophy, and who will need to be in wheelchairs their entire lives. When the oldest child got his first wheelchair, his dad, Ryan asked what he wanted to be for Halloween. "A pirate!" was the enthusiastic response. So Ryan created not just a pirate costume, but a whole ship to fit around the wheelchair. It got a lot of attention, and was just the beginning of a journey of fantastic costumes for his kids, which has grown into the non-profit. Magic Wheelchair chooses 5 children a year, who submit a video of what they would like their costume to be, and creates costumes for them at no cost to the child's family. What a great way of identifying a need, and reaching out to a community that has often been forgotten in the realm of costumes. What if you were to expand on their idea and make costumes for adults in wheelchairs?

One of the coolest things I've ever seen came from some friends of mine over at Bloodlust Productions who are some of the most ridiculously creative and talented people that I have had the honor of meeting. I don't think this is their regular production line, but I think it totally should be. They made a zombie dog pet costume for a little Chihuahua. It was all bloody and gnarly and gross and I thought it was the most brilliant thing I've ever seen. Because I realized, for people who are like us and real big into Halloween, we may not want to dress our dog up like a ladybug one more time. There are all kinds of cutesy costumes for pets but what about creepy, freaky, or weird costumes? Or, someone asked me fairly recently, what about costumes for exotic pets? I think he was joking; he was like, "What about my snake?" I don't know if you can get a snake to wear a costume but who knows, maybe so! The point is, there is a lot of room for creativity in this area and there's stuff that hasn't been done yet. I think whenever you can blaze a new trail it's a good thing. People crave novelty- it garners interest, and draws people to you. So if you're into costumes and you're into pets go for it.

Let's take a minute to talk about masks, which are a segment of costumes. I'm part of a Facebook group that's called Sculptors/Mask makers/Makeup artists and there are just some amazing things out there. Because there has been trouble with spammers, the group is closed, but if you are interested, (and not a spammer!) send a request to join. There's room for all kinds of creativity and you can do pretty masks, scary masks, or something in-between. You could probably have a whole business just doing scary clown masks! A word of caution though, this is an area with tremendous competition! Be aware that you will need to really on top of your game to break into this market. This means being creative, on top of trends, willing to customize, adjust, and grow as an artist. Be unique- don't rip other people's ideas off. That is the number one complaint among mask makers that I've spoken with.

You could create atmosphere DVDs, CD's, and MP3's for people to play at their parties or at their home haunts. There's a few out there but there could always be more, especially if you can figure out a way to make something better or improve it. If you find yourself looking at one of these atmosphere DVDs that's in existence and you think, "That's kind of boring, I could do it better!" Well, do it! Start by booking time in a local recording studio. Get a group of film students together to show you how to use the equipment. Hire an editor to make your recording, whether it is sound or video, the best it can be.

Another thing you could make is calendars. There's a fun one called, "Gory and Gorgeous" and the Hauntforum Home Haunt calendar which are definitely more a niche thing. However, I think there's enough interest out there that there could be more than one of these kinds of calendars. A calendar idea I've had for a while is, "A Skelly For All Seasons". The idea got into my head when I saw pictures somebody had posted a couple of years ago right after Halloween. Someone had put a Santa hat on their jack-o-lantern and skeletons in their yard and I thought, "How funny is that?" There are people who don't want to take down their Halloween decorations but they also want to decorate for Christmas. How fun would it be if you had a calendar that was a skeleton in your yard for every month of the year? For example, in January you could dress them up like baby New Year and then in February you could have them be cupid and so on, you get the idea. I just think that would be a blast to put together! There's a great picture I saw recently that said: Halloween it's not just a holiday, it's a lifestyle. What you would want to be looking at all throughout the year to keep you in the Halloween spirit and in the mood, what could be fun?

Making candles is an option that can involve high start-up costs and requires patience, practice, and skill. I used to work for Jerry Hurst, of The Royal Candlemaker at the New York and Texas Renaissance festivals, who made scenery candles with Halloween figurines. He also made carved candles in custom colors (which you could get or make ones in Halloween colors. For lifestyle Halloween and Goth enthusiasts, he made castle candles that could definitely be left up all year long.

There is also a great candle company named Dark Candles that offers all sorts of great sets of scented candles. On top of having a Halloween scented line including such scents as Carnival, Falling Leaves, and Jack-o-Lantern, they also have Crypt Moss, Coffin, Dracula, and all sorts of great creepy scents that are fantastic.

Speaking of scents, there are a few companies out there like Froggy's Fog and Sinister Scents, who have developed a line of scents for professional haunts. These companies noticed that the olfactory aspect of the experience was often lacking, so they created products to fill the need. Most of their scents are on the super gross, stinky side, (like Slaughterhouse, Rotting Decay, Swampy Marsh) and are not really something you'd want for your house or home haunt, but it is a great example of a niche product!

Let's talk about home furnishings. Again, this will likely be for your lifestyle folks. You could make or sell blankets, quilts, dinnerware (plates, goblets, candelabras, et cetera) pillows, bookends, lamps, statuary, or knick-knacks. This could be for people who want a little bit of Halloween all the time but not the cheap, cheesy, tacky stuff that they got at the Dollar Store for year round use. If you're really into quilting, how about designing patterns and/or kits for beautiful, dark quilts? There are a lot of cutesy Halloween quilts out there, but what about people who want to hang something beautiful on their wall, or cuddle beneath a scary monster quilt? Or maybe a beautiful, dark landscape artwork quilt? What if you made a Halloween t-shirt quilt, or one made out of old, beloved costumes? If you put together a beautiful quality product or make the kit, people will buy it.

Next up are paper products such as invitations, greeting cards and stationary: this is kind of a fun niche to get into. If you're a designer or an artist there are some great websites available to you such as Zazzle.com, where you can put your artwork out there and not have to do all the product manufacturing yourself. Wrapping paper and gift bags are along those same lines. Like I pointed out before, you wouldn't even need to concentrate on selling to retail buyers or consumers. You could sell to businesses (such as card or stationary stores and websites) who will resell your products.

Let's not forget clothing. Now we're talking apparel here (not costumes), such as t-shirts, socks, gloves, arm warmers, and that sort of thing. While I was at the Halloween Party Expo, I talked to TheMountain.com, a wholesaler of t-shirts. They had a wide variety of great artwork and I asked where they got it all from. I explained that I'm a small business idea consultant and I work with a lot of artists and designers who have great work. Often, they would like to put their designs on t-shirts and other products, but they don't know how to get started beyond cafépress.com. They told me that artists can submit work to them for consideration and the company will take care of the manufacturing and sales. The artist then gets paid royalties on every shirt sold. The resources are out there, you don't have to do it all yourself.

This next one is one of my personal favorites: Music! Music is another great thing to add atmosphere to parties. You can sell either MP3 or CDs and again you can create and sell atmospheric music. Also, there are a number of bands who perform regular fun, spooky songs like Creature Feature, Wednesday 13, and Ghouls Night Out. They're always a little kitschy, a little fun, and it's a great way to share entertainment. I will address music further in the Entertainment and Performance section.

What would Halloween be without pumpkins? Later, I'll be talking about renting land to grow and sell pumpkins, but for products, let's look beyond just the actual fruit. Earlier we talked about Ray Villafane's "Mr. Potato Head" products but there are more opportunities out there. What might you do differently than the vine arms and legs? Pumpkin Masters have been offering awesome jack-o-lantern carving templates for years, and have expanded their line to include carving tools. Recently, I had a chance to talk with Jim Christopherson of PumpkinWow, who identified a way to improve on the carving templates, and solve the problem of hole-poking fatigue. He invented a template that acts like a temporary tattoo and eliminates the time spent on poking holes before you carve. I watched as he used a Dremel® to carve several of his designs into Funkins ®. The process was indeed easy and fast. If I had any experience with power tools, I would have loved to have given it a shot! He told me about how he took one of his designs, a creepy zombie football player's face to a pro football game and sold the finished product (on a Funkin ®) as fast as he could make them, for $150 each. Think you could hone your skills enough to be able to do something like that?

The last topic in the products chapter is reserved for decorations. Decorations are a huge segment of the Halloween industry and so if you love to make some sort of decoration, there's room for you there. Think about whether you would want to focus on indoor or outdoor decorations, and, who do you want to be buying them.

Two things that I'm not seeing people talk a whole lot about are specialty foods and beverage and wedding supplies. The specialty foods and beverages market is a wide open field. Vampire wine or similarly themed drinks is a big thing. Maybe you could design a gory shots guide. There was an artist in Thailand named Kittiwat Unarrom who made bread body parts. I don't think he's doing it anymore, but Google it. It is phenomenally gross! But if they sold them here in the states I would probably buy them (at least once!). He made breads to look like gnarled faces or fake hands or feet. Then he would decorate them with I'm guessing either food coloring or jellies to make them look bloody and gross. It is so creative. Again, this is not going to be a mainstream thing but would probably be a big hit at parties or for your year-round Halloween enthusiasts. Kaci Hansen, The Homicidal Homemaker, has a delightful blog and Youtube channel dedicated to fun, gross looking recipes and party ideas. As of this writing, she will soon have a cooking show available through Roku (and other channels) as well as a book featuring her recipes. What if you were to put together your own recipes and sell them to magazines to publish in their fall/October issues?

In Services we talked about holding cooking classes to teach folks to make healthy Halloween treats, but what about the people who just don't have time to learn? You could just provide healthy (or healthier) treats to shops; make them available for parties (maybe even partner up with a caterer or party planner?)

So Halloween weddings are becoming a big thing and that could actually span all seven categories, but for the moment we're going to focus on products. People are going to want really unique Halloween weddings and if you can create delightfully dark wedding supplies likes invitations, favors, cakes, decorations, and table toppers, all the things that go into experiencing a wedding, you will never lack for business. This kind of custom work is something people who are looking for an outside-the-box wedding will happily pay for. They will be super excited to find someone who understands them, and who won't try to talk them into a cookie-cutter, seen-in-the-latest-issue of a magazine wedding. Please go to my website, www.beweirdmakemoney.com for a more in-depth discussion on Halloween weddings.

I know dollhouses aren't enjoying the same kind of popularity they once did, but after I did a Google search for Halloween dollhouses that returned 420,000 hits I realized there may be a lot of people searching for this kind of product. What if you made a Haunted House series of dollhouse miniatures? It could be along the lines of Lenox's Spooky Town. Or, if not scary, maybe super-cutesy or vintage-style miniatures that recall an earlier era of Halloween? You could try both, and see what appeals more.

An area of intangible products are phone apps. There are some great ones out there, like HauntFinder and Findahaunt.com , which lists the names, locations, and other vital information of haunted attractions near you. What if you expanded that to include all kinds of Halloween happenings in your area? It could be a free app, but maybe you could charge people a few dollars who want their event to be listed? This may or may not be a big money maker, but it could bring in some extra money for you. Another thing you might do, although it will require some research, is to make it sort of a syndicated app for several different areas. That would widen the pool of possible advertisers and up your

.

earning potential. If it proves to be popular, you might

consider doing it for that OTHER big holiday that

follows closely after Halloween. *wink

Chapter Four: Information

Information is great because it allows you to be creative; there's no geographic limit thanks to the internet. You can repackage your information once you put it together. For example, if you do a presentation, you could have it transcribed and sell it as books or reports. You could write a series of articles or blog posts that you then put together as a book. The coolest part is that it doesn't even necessarily have to be your information. You don't have to create it from scratch. Now I don't want you to go plagiarize, but there is plenty of free public domain information out there that you could put together. It takes some time to track down the free information, but that is where the money is. Most people don't have the patience or interest to do the research, but if you pull all that information together and put it out there, there are people who would be willing to buy it. Use your personal experience to put a list of, "Here's when you need liability insurance and here's when you don't", "Ten things Fire Department officials are going to look for", or, "Ten things to minimize your liability". These examples are mostly geared towards home haunters, but whatever information you want to put together, it's out there.

Putting together how-to DVDs may not necessarily sell because there's so much free information out there on the internet, but you might be able to sell that information with a kit. Most likely some people will only be willing track down one part of the idea, like a video, but would fizzle out after that. If you put everything together for this prop or this costume so that people just have to assemble, you would draw in the crafty people who don't necessarily know how to create something from scratch; they're going to love it. When we do "make-and-takes" with my Garage of Evil group, we'll pick a prop to make and whoever's hosting will put together kits for everyone. Then all we have to do is walk in, hand them a check, and it's all right there for us which is great. Some popular topics are props, makeup, or costume making. What if you made a series of videos and kits, and made it into a subscription service? Speaking of subscription services, what about putting together a service like Horror Block, which is a monthly delivery service that sends out things like horror-related t-shirts, toys, and posters? Or got sponsored by manufacturers to demonstrate their products?

Also you could monetize your blog using ads and affiliate programs. Maybe consider doing a video series or a pod cast where you would tie-in the kits. For example, show a how-to on your video or pod cast, on how to make a really cool tombstone, pneumatic prop or something like that. At the end make the offer, "If you want to make this prop, you can order my all-inclusive kit for $49.95".

Or what about this- You may not think of it this way, but wherever you are is a destination for someone. What if you made a little guide, list, or article about all the Halloween goings-on in your town and call it something like "Destination Halloween In *Your Town*!" You could submit it to local or online media sites. You could also ask Halloween attractions or related businesses if they'd be willing to pay you to be featured. Your town doesn't need to be Salem, Massachusetts or New Orleans, Louisiana to be considered interesting!

Chapter Five: Landlord

Now I don't want to freak anyone out. I don't know if you or someone close to you has ever owned real estate and had renters that became a cautionary tale; this isn't like that. Basically I want to expand your thinking about what the word "landlord" can mean. You want to be renting things (or spaces) to people who don't want to own them. This can happen anywhere and it's a way that allows your stuff to support you instead of you supporting your stuff. This is one of those areas that not everyone is thinking of yet and it's a great way to start thinking differently. Here is where you could rent out old props. Say you used to have a home haunt and your theme was witch doctor. You had a haunted island and all sorts of creepy props for that. But after a couple of years you decide to do a carnival theme. Well what are you going to do with all of those props- throw them out? Probably not; I hope not! You might be able to repurpose some of them, but what if you held on to them to rent out to people who wanted to have a theme like yours? If you have an over-abundance of tombstones, what if you were able to rent some of those out? (Or is that just me? Ha! Because I think you can never have enough tombstones!) You could also build props with the intent to rent them- like if you're getting started with decorating other people's yards or you know someone who is. There's a company in Los Angeles, California, called Dapper Cadaver and that's exactly what they do. They rent out movie quality props to local businesses. Now, they're in Los Angeles, so you're probably not going to want to rent from them if you live in Bangor, Maine. So what if there was somebody local doing that at movie quality? If there were, you can imagine they probably would not be within most people's budgets. You could compete with that company by creating props that are good quality but at an affordable price. Then you would have bigger pool of people who would be willing to rent from you. You could also rent out your decorated house or space for parties and events. Do you have access to a barn or a warehouse or an office space that you could rent out once it's all decorated? Because again, you might only have one party for the season but then your space would be decorated and you would have the opportunity to make your entertaining budget back. You may not want to invite the general public in, but if you know of a couple of people (or organizations) who also want to have parties, then you could rent out your space. Now there might be some liability issues, so make sure to check with your insurance carrier. However, it could be a way to support your Halloween habit by using something that you've already got.

Another way to approach this landlord idea would be the reverse, to find places to rent that haven't even considered renting, such as off-season areas (camps/towns). What about places like summer camps and summer towns that shut down at Labor Day? What if you worked with them to provide additional, off-season income by making it a Halloween destination?

If it is a camp, maybe you could offer a Live Action Role Playing event that features a horror themed game, treasure hunt, or zombie paintball (probably only if the camp hold paintball during regular season, though- it's kind of messy!) What if you made a kid-friendly version during the day and an 18+ version for night time? That's double the revenue, and serves twice as many people. Or, you could have a side-by-side set of encounters for both groups simultaneously. You could appeal to new groups as well as the regular patrons of the camp. What makes this different from traditional Haunted attractions is its interactivity. At regular haunts you are most likely just walking through a warren of scary rooms and encounters. With this idea, people would be involved in solving puzzles, finding things- maybe you could even encourage or provide costumes and makeup as part of the fun (and price!).

If it is a tourist town (like a seaside town or a mountain ski area), coordinate with the year-round local shops and come up with a sort of incentive package to draw people in during the slow times. Maybe it would look like a one day or Halloween-themed weekend carnival. Or draw on (or create) ghost stories and legends of the area.

As you'll find out later in the book, I do not have a green thumb or a place to grow things even if I did. This is why, like millions of other people, I purchase my pumpkin from one of many local farms offering them. But what if (unlike me) you can actually make a garden grow? What if you have a big piece of property that is otherwise vacant, but could be used to grow crops? Why not rent your land to grow pumpkins- to one person who shares profit/pays rent or as a community garden, where interested people would pay a small fee to use that space to grow their pumpkins? If you don't have the land, do you know someone that you could partner with and split

the profits?

Chapter Six: Mail Order

Mail order is great because it's a global, so geography becomes irrelevant. If you live in the middle of nowhere Idaho, but you want to have a business, this is a great way to do it. Now this can either be snail mail order, internet, (such as having a shop on Etsy or eBay), or just your own website. Also, if you work with drop shippers you could not only have a relatively low start-up cost, but you would not have to worry about ordering, holding stock, or dealing with customer service. You could put a site together and see who's interested in what. Everyone has seen different websites and catalogs; some of my favorites include Grandin Road's Halloween Haven, Fright Catalog, and Fright Props. Another untapped niche you could fill might be putting together a catalog of mom and pop products! What I'm talking about is people creating these little cottage industries in their house or garage. What if you put a catalog together of products that these folks are making? Everyone can go onto Spirit, Fright Catalog, or Grandin Road's website and buy mass produced things- which is great because they have awesome things. But there's this whole other side of the business that's not being addressed; I think people really want to buy handmade things or small batch products. So what if you didn't have to make any of it, you just have to find the people who are creating great things and show them a way to get those things in front of customers? You could put them all in one space for people to find.

Another option is gift baskets. Gift baskets are a wonderful business idea for any time of year and for any interest. I remember seeing one a couple years ago called Goth Gift Baskets in Gothic Beauty Magazine. It was all sorts of dark products that they would put in really cool black baskets with black tissue paper and silver ribbons. I got to thinking, "Wouldn't it be fun to send your favorite Halloween enthusiast a fun gift basket full of Halloween goodies? You could fill it with candles, candy, and vampire wine? All this would be a really interesting way to either add to your business if you already do something like gift baskets or it could be a seasonal thing. You could get featured in a niche magazine like Haunted Attraction Magazine, Rue Morgue, Fangoria, Makeup Artist, Gothic Beauty, Cemetery Dance, or just seasonal issues of mainstream magazines like Woman's Day or Martha Stewart's annual Halloween issue. Just think about how people would find you. A great way to get them talking is to get it out there where people are reading.

If you have a love of sifting, sorting, and restoring, you could specialize in Halloween antiques or antiques with a haunted history.

To be honest, this next idea is something that never occurred to me until I saw a news story about it over the summer. Hear me out because this is a little weird (even for me!): Mail decorated pumpkins- probably mini ones. The fine folks over at mailaspud.com charge $10 to mail a potato, with or without a message, to the person of your choosing. They make over $10,000 a month. No really. Check out their website. They have a great sense of humor. Clearly, pumpkins are a very seasonal item,

but who says this has to be a year round gig for you?

Chapter Seven: Bricks and Mortar

Bricks and mortar has relatively high start-up costs. You have to be really committed to your idea even if you're only doing it seasonally. For example, you could be seasonal like Spirit who comes in for three months a year and does their thing and then packs up and heads out. Or you could have a year round business depending on what you want to do. Do you want to put in a lot of investment and get a lot of return for a short period of time? Or do you want to have something that sustains you through the year?

One idea for a bricks and mortar business might be haunt themed mini-golf. I don't know where you are in the country but I know there's a nationwide franchise called

Monster Golf. There's one local to me and I've been a couple of times and I love it! Basically it's a glow in the dark mini-golf that has animatronics and props and paintings of different haunt themed things. Like, there's one hole where you hit the ball and Frankenstein pops up out of a coffin. It's a lot of fun but it's basically designed for kids, so it's a little scary but not enough to cause trauma. What if you designed one that was more adult themed? What if it was a seasonal thing attached to one of your local haunts, as a way to make more money at the haunt? It could be something for people who came with friends but decided they don't want to do the haunt walk-through. Or if there's a huge line they can go play a round of mini-golf while they're waiting.

You could have a makeup and/or costume shop. This could sustain you throughout the year, for example, if you had local theatrical groups or cosplayers as regular customers. There are all kinds of events (like Comicons, Anime conventions, Renaissance festivals) that happen throughout the year that folks will need and want costumes, wigs, and makeup for.

What about a boutique of mom and pop stuff, again kind of like with the catalog idea? What if you had that in a retail storefront? And you could mix it in with mass produced stuff and that way you'd have the best of both worlds.

I don't know if you've ever been to New York City, but there is a company called Eerie Entertainment. At one point they had several theme restaurants/pubs open-think Hard Rock Café or Planet Hollywood only it was horror themed things. The restaurants that are still open are the Jekyll and Hyde Pub and the Slaughtered Lamb Pub. There used to be the Jekyll and Hyde Club, The Night Gallery and the Jack the Ripper Pub but I think these last three have closed down. But you go in and it's this full on experience where the wait staff is all dressed up and in character. To find the bathroom in the one location, it's a bookcase and you have to find the hidden book that is the door- ha! It was such a fun experience to go and I thought, "Wow! We really need one of these in Colorado." So why not in your state, too- if Eerie Entertainment isn't available as a franchise, why not start your own themed restaurant?

Also I saw a thread on HauntForum a couple of years ago from somebody who had a bed and breakfast. In the month of October they really decorated it heavy duty, they "haunted it" they said, and I thought, "How brilliant is that?" What if you got together with a local bed and breakfast owner (you don't have to own the bed and breakfast) and teamed up with them and helped them decorate? You could even see if they wanted your help during the month, if it significantly increases business. That's a way that you can be involved with the bricks and mortar business without having to own it which is always a good thing!

Murder mystery dinners are nothing new, but what about ones with a specific haunted, supernatural, or Halloween theme? You could seek out a place that is already set up to do the dinners, and work with them to provide the stories, props, actors, whatever they need most, to host them from mid-September to mid-October. This would be a great alternative for folks who don't like haunted attractions- either for the prices, being too scary, or too short. It doesn't mean the storyline(s) have to be boring, just not the kind of over-the-top, jump scares that haunted attractions rely on.

Chapter Eight: Entertainment or Performance

Entertainment or performance is always a fun topic. Entertainment is great because if you're really creative, like I'm guessing you are, it's a way to channel that. There are options that are good for both introverts and extraverts, depending on what you're choosing to do. There will be mixed start-up costs, but there's usually an affordable way to get into it. Most of these ideas are portable, where you go different places and you perform or entertain. If you are an introvert you can send things out, like writing pieces. Some things that these might look like are: haunt actor or haunt line entertainment. Haunt line entertainment is a mixed bag in my experience. I think they could step it up. Anyone can juggle chainsaws; I want to see severed heads being juggled!

You could hire yourself out as a story teller to kid's parties or other events and tell ghost stories, creepy stories, either originals or classics. One haunt in New Jersey had a "Haunted Fairy Tale Forest" theme, and they had had their line snaked through the woods. Their storyteller was placed along the path and told stories from a huge book prop in her lap as people waited. You could take that idea and make a character out of it- think Creepy Mother Goose or John Hurt's character in Jim Henson's TV show "The Storyteller".

I alluded to this before in products, but you could either be a live musician or you could be a DJ and provide atmosphere music. Nox Arcana and Midnight Syndicate do a great job with atmospheric soundtracks. Other bands like the Rockabilly/Gothabilly bands like Psycho Charger, Creature Feature, Ghoul's Night Out and Voltaire are great examples of fun, somewhat novelty music that is in a similar spirit to Halloween classic artists like John Zacherle or Bobby "Boris" Pickett. As a DJ you could either focus on events or create an online radio station. Sites like Live 365 have some really great Halloween stations and a fairly straightforward way to get started. Music Macabre is one of my favorite Live365 stations. Along with Musique Macabre, Halloweenradio.net always finds really great songs I had no idea existed and it really adds to my enjoyment as a Halloween enthusiast. I can turn on these radio stations

24/7, 365 days a year and listen to Halloween music. It's great!

You could be an alternative model or an evil clown for hire. I read this story last year about a guy in Sweden who hired himself out as an evil clown. Parents would apparently hire this guy to creep their kids out the week before their birthday. Now I'm not into child trauma but I couldn't stop laughing when I read that. My niece is terrified of clowns and I thought if that guy was in New Jersey I would totally hire him! You could hire yourself out as an evil clown to do photo bombs or just show up at places to freak people out. If you start thinking really big, you could have a whole franchise of evil clowns for hire. Think like the mall Santa Claus industry, with clowns able to be hired out for parties, photo bombs, etc.

There is a guy called Lizard Man and he has really capitalized on his need to be weird. He has done all sorts of body modification to look like a lizard. He's had bone implants, tattoos and he even had his tongue bifurcated. He's kind of amazing. He performs music, writes, and hires himself out for parties; he has really diverse income streams. If you like the thought of doing that, but aren't sure about the commitment to do all the body modification, you don't have to do that. You could just do makeup and be an interesting character for people to hire for parties.

If you are an author, you could write novels, short stories, or magazine articles. There are a number of magazines that are dedicated just to horror literature such as Shroud, Cemetery Dance or the Alfred Hitchcock magazine. Now they're not necessarily looking for Halloween themed pieces, but definitely thriller or mystery. There's also room in a lot of Halloween issues for creative input. There are also anthologies of Halloween short stories; Cemetery Dance put one out a couple of years ago called October Dreams, personally it's one of my favorite books. There are a lot of horror anthologies out there but there's very few that have to do with Halloween specifically. Kind of like how there's a lot of horror movies but there's not a ton of movies for Halloween. When "Trick 'r Treat" came out a couple of years ago it was such a delight because it was simply about Halloween (secretly, I watched it 3 times the day I bought the DVD!). That's another thing; making movies or screenwriter. There's so much television that's geared towards horror now – that's really opening up and they could probably use some great Halloween ideas.

Being a voiceover actor is another option. Dick Terhune has a great program teaching people how to do voiceover acting for creepy productions which would be a lot of fun. You could offer your services via fiverr.com or to local businesses to do their seasonal commercials. Here is where Fiverr is a perfect example of how to start small, and try your idea(s) out before going big time.

If you are a photographer, you could hire yourself out for parties and large events to capture people in their costumes. As an add-on, you could offer vanity books for people to remember the event. When I was at HauntCon and the Halloween Party Expo there was a booth that would take a picture of you in front a green screen. They had a few Halloween themed backgrounds for you to choose to put behind you and your friends. They sold a printout for you take home. That is one idea to add extra revenue to your mix.

Chapter Nine: How to Become

Ubiquitous

Here's something my mentor Barbara Winter calls "How to Become Ubiquitous" Ubiquitous is such a fun word which means *"appearing to be in many places at once."* The concept of becoming ubiquitous is basically taking one of the ideas we talked about and turning it into multiple profit centers. If you have one idea that you really love, you might be able to stretch it over a whole bunch of different businesses. That way, some of the businesses might be bringing in money at times and sometimes others will. This is a great way to make yours a diversified, sustaining lifestyle business. If one area of your business isn't bringing in money, another might.

I would like to show you an example of how you could make one idea ubiquitous. I came up with a set of ideas that couple of years ago. It's not necessarily Halloween – based, but it's related, and is a very good illustration of the concept of branching out an idea. Now you might remember my mentioning my lack of gardening skills earlier. It's a little ironic that despite the fact that I've been known to kill plastic plants, I came up with a business plan design around gardening! However, I thought this would be a great idea for someone who can actually grow things.

Gothic gardening: I got the inspiration from a website by the same name put together back in the late '90's by someone called Malice in Wonderland. They had the most fabulous list of theme gardens: gardening to attract bats, night blooming gardens, or gardens to attract fairies. There were naturally occurring dark red flowers, black flowers, and purple flowers among the lists of theme gardens. I thought, "How cool could this be?" I just loved the site and when I got thinking about how one idea could straddle all of these different lines of businesses, Gothic Gardening seemed a good place to start.

> **_Services:_** You could do-over people's gardens, for people like me who don't know how to garden. As the client, I could say, "I want a garden full of dark red and night blooming flowers." And you as the landscape architect could come in, design and create it in the space I have available.

Products: You could either design or find people who design things like garden statuary, creepy weeping angels, that sort of thing. Or maybe you could put together starter kits of seeds and seedlings. Maybe this is another theme that you could add to your gift baskets. You could do arrangements of beautiful dark flowers in skull vases.

Information: You could have a blog or a book or a web based garden design program, so you're not necessarily stuck if you live in the middle of nowhere. You could do this if you're good at landscape design and you could do this from anywhere. People could send you pictures of their garden and get consultations on your design ideas.

Then you just design a plan for them, email it to them and get paid. Maybe you could even get them hooked up with local businesses, like plant nurseries or landscapers, who could help make it happen.

Landlord: Once you have established a really awesome garden, you could rent it out for pictures or events. It could be where all the Goth kids go to get their prom pictures or senior portraits done.

Mail order: You could put together a catalog of your products. You know- the seeds, seedlings, statuary, and starter kits.

Entertainment: You could have a TV show, blog, or pod cast of transforming people's gardens.

Think 'Extreme Home Makeovers', but instead creeping out someone's garden. Remember when HGTV used to have actual gardening shows? It could be like that. Since it's not really mainstream you would just probably have it on the web, but it would be available for your target market.

Bricks and Mortar: If you have an established garden, you could make it into a botanical garden where people could come and just enjoy your different themes. Then, you could have a tea house where people could sit and enjoy tea and light refreshments while enjoying creepy statuary surrounded by black flowers. You could invite local musicians to play for your guests, or the musicians could rent your space for album release parties. It could also become a perfect Goth or Halloween wedding reception destination. How fun would that be?

<u>Conclusion</u>

So, who's ready to get started? Hopefully I've gotten the gears going and the synapses firing for all the different ideas of what you'd like to do.

Now you can justify your year round Halloween obsession so you don't have to hide stuff from your spouse when you buy Halloween goodies. If you're making money at it I bet your family would leave you alone, even if they still don't quite understand it. You could make more money to afford more Halloween stuff; or maybe you don't want to replace your income. Maybe you just want more money to buy better swag. But, if this is something that you've really been holding onto, this is the time to get your dream started. Get recognition for your talent and being the creative person that I know you are!

I'd really love to chat with you if you have questions or want to discuss anything I talked about in this book. The thing I love to do most in life is explore ideas and adding Halloween is just the cherry on top, it's wonderful. I look forward to hearing from you. Stay spooky!

P.S. Please check out my website www.beweirdmakemoney.com for material that didn't make it into this edition of the book! You will also find information about my individual consulting, webinars, and workshops opportunities there as well.

www.ingramcontent.com/pod-product-compliance
Lightning Source LLC
Chambersburg PA
CBHW022109170526
45157CB00004B/1558